JESUS
IN ME

STUDY GUIDE

For more resources by Anne Graham Lotz visit
www.annegrahamlotz.org

JESUS IN ME

Experiencing *the* Holy Spirit *as a* Constant Companion

STUDY GUIDE

EIGHT SESSIONS

ANNE GRAHAM LOTZ

Harper*Christian* Resources

CONTENTS

ABOUT
ANNE GRAHAM LOTZ

CALLED "THE BEST PREACHER IN THE FAMILY" by her father, Billy Graham, Anne Graham Lotz speaks around the globe with the wisdom and authority of years spent studying God's Word.

The *New York Times* named Anne one of the five most influential evangelists of her generation. She's been profiled on *60 Minutes* and has appeared on TV programs such as *Larry King Live, The Today Show,* and *Hannity Live.* Her Just Give Me Jesus revivals have been held in more than thirty cities in twelve different countries, to hundreds of thousands of attendees.

Whether a delegate to Davos' Economic Forum, a commentator to the *Washington Post*, or a groundbreaking speaker on platforms throughout the world, Anne's aim is clear—to bring revival to the hearts of God's people. And her message is consistent—calling people into a personal relationship with God through His Word and through prayer.

In May 2016, Anne was named the Chairperson of the National Day of Prayer Task Force, a position held by only two other women, Shirley Dobson and Vonette Bright, since its inception in 1952.

Anne is a bestselling and award-winning author. Her most recent releases are *The Light of His Presence, Jesus in Me, The Daniel Prayer, Wounded by God's People, Fixing My Eyes on Jesus, Expecting to See Jesus*, and her first children's book, *Heaven: God's Promise for Me.*

Anne and her late husband, Danny Lotz, have three grown children and three grandchildren. She is the founder and president of AnGeL Ministries, an independent, non-profit organization based in Raleigh, North Carolina, that is committed to giving out messages of biblical exposition so God's Word is personal and relevant to ordinary people.

The ministry's name is derived from the initials of Anne Graham Lotz (AGL) and is especially fitting, as angels are messengers of God who go wherever He sends, speak to whomever He directs, and faithfully deliver His Word. AnGeL Ministries serves as the umbrella organization for the diverse ministry of Anne Graham Lotz—including her many books, DVDs, CDs, speaking engagements, and special events.

To learn more about Anne and AnGeL Ministries, visit
www.annegrahamlotz.org.

PREFACE

Recently I went to the ENT doctor because I thought I had reached the stage of needing hearing aids. The doctor tested me, then concluded, "Mrs. Lotz, you don't need hearing aids because you have virtually no hearing loss. Your problem is that you don't listen." I couldn't help but laugh because I knew he was right! When I'm tired or busy, I don't always pay attention to someone who is speaking. And if the person is fairly long-winded, my mind will wander to other things. As a result, I'm disconnected. Distracted. Even though I hear the sound of the voice, I don't know what's being said because I'm not listening.

The same thing is true when it comes to reading my Bible. I can read the words, yet not really hear what God is saying because I'm rushing through my reading, or distracted by wandering thoughts, or focused only on facts and information, or just too tired to concentrate. As a result, my daily time with Him in His Word becomes routine. Drudgery. A "have-to," not a "want-to" exercise.

Learning to listen for God's voice speaking to me through the pages of my Bible has transformed my daily time with Him. I now approach the time with eager anticipation of what He will say. Perhaps more than any other aspect of my Christian life, it has drawn me closer to Him in an intimate relationship. It has become the very core of who I am. Because, dear friend, God *does* speak through His Word. I *know* . . .!

This video Bible study, *Jesus in Me*, is designed to teach you how to listen to the whispers of the Holy Spirit as you read God's Word. It has been patterned after my own daily devotional exercise. I'm excited for you to discover the joy of hearing God's voice speaking to you personally as you learn to listen.

Every blessing,

Anne Graham Lotz

ABOUT THE STUDY

THIS STUDY GUIDE IS TO BE USED WITH the video-based course *Jesus in Me: Experiencing the Holy Spirit as a Constant Companion*. As an integral part of the course, it provides a format for Bible study that serves as the basis for both small group use (Sunday school classes, women's or men's groups, home or neighborhood studies, one-on-one discipleship) and individual use. This guide will lead you through a series of questions that will enable you to not only discover for yourself the eternal truths revealed by God in the Bible, but also to hear God speaking personally to you through His Word. You then will be prepared to participate in a meaningful time of study and discussion with members of your small group.

INDIVIDUAL STUDY

Each week you will work through 5 Bible studies on selected passages of Scripture using the 3-question steps you will learn during the workshop in session 1. Before you meet with your group, be sure to take the time to reflect and record your *Live in Obedient Response* statements to share with your group so they can encourage you and hold you accountable.

It is important to complete each individual study before your next session, as this will make the video presentation more meaningful to you during the small group time. Note that meaningful, daily Bible study will occur if you:

- Set aside a regular place for private devotions.
- Set aside a regular time for private devotions.
- Pray before beginning the day's assignment, asking God to speak to you through His Word.

- Write out your answers for each step, in sequence.
- Make the time to be still and listen, reflecting thoughtfully on your response in the final step.
- Don't rush—it may take time in prayerful meditation on a given passage to discover meaningful lessons and hear the Spirit's whispers.

Spiritual discipline is an essential part of your ability to grow in your relationship with God through knowledge and understanding of His Word. So, take your individual study seriously and allow God to speak to you from His Word.

GROUP STUDY

Note: Each session will require approximately 60 minutes of group meeting time to share the discoveries from Individual Bible study, watch the video, and discuss the teaching and content.

You will review the lessons, personal applications, and take-aways at the beginning of your group meeting and then watch the teaching from Anne. After each video teaching, there will be group discussion time to learn from one another and share in the experience of the Holy Spirit as a constant companion.

In session 1 of *Jesus In Me*, you will watch the video workshop and be introduced to the 3-question Bible study method. You will use John 14:15–20 during the workshop to help you better understand this approach. (Note that if your group meets less frequently than once a week, you may want to extend your study time for each passage.)

Space is provided for you to take notes during the video presentation. After the message, you will then have time to discuss the key concepts with your small group using the questions in this guide.

Note: If you are the facilitator for the group, there are additional instructions and resources provided in the back of this study guide. This guide will help you structure your meeting time, facilitate discussion times, and help you lead group members through the key points of the study.

INDIVIDUAL COMMITMENT

Remember that the real growth in this study will happen during your quiet times with God during the week. During the group times, you will have the opportunity to process what you have learned with the other members, ask questions, and learn from them as you listen to what God is doing in their lives. In addition, keep in mind that the videos, discussions, and activities in this study are simply meant to tune your heart and your spiritual ears to God's voice so that you can live out what He says as you grow closer to Him.

BIBLE STUDY
WORKSHOP

THIS BIBLE STUDY WORKSHOP has a single purpose: to present an approach that will help you learn to listen for God's voice, know Him in a personal relationship, and communicate with Him through His Word. The following information is introduced in detail in the video presentation. Use this section of the study guide as you view the workshop material. Underline key thoughts and take additional notes as you participate in the workshop. (Note that the passages Anne uses as examples in the video workshop are found on pages 6–7.)

WHAT YOU NEED

Before you begin the video workshop for this first session, you will need the following:

- ❏ a Bible
- ❏ this study guide
- ❏ pen or pencil
- ❏ time
- ❏ prayer
- ❏ an open heart

WATCH VIDEO SESSION 1 (49 MINUTES)

Anne will use this video session to walk you through the following 5 Steps to Bible study with the 3 questions that are essential to the Bible Study Workshop. She will illustrate how to do this Bible study with Colossians 1:26–27 (see pages 6–7 in your study guide).

STEPS TO BIBLE STUDY

STEP 1: READ GOD'S WORD
(Look at the Passage.)

The first step is to *read the Bible.* At the start of each session in this study guide, you will find the Scriptures listed in a column that you should read during the week. When you have finished reading the passage for the day, move on to Step 2.

STEP 2: WHAT DOES GOD'S WORD SAY?
(List the Facts.)

After reading the passage, make a verse-by-verse list of the outstanding facts. Don't get caught up in the details—just pinpoint the most obvious facts as they appear to you. When you make your list, do not paraphrase the text but use actual words from the passage. Look for the nouns and the verbs.

STEP 3: WHAT DOES GOD'S WORD MEAN?
(Learn the Lessons.)

After reading the passage and listing the facts, look for a lesson to learn from each fact. Ask yourself the following questions:

- *Who is speaking?*

- *What is the subject?*

- *Where is it taking place?*

- *When did it happen?*

- *What can I learn from what is taking place or what is being said?*

It may also help to ask yourself: *What are the people in the passage doing that I should be doing? Is there a command I should obey? A promise I should claim? A warning I should heed? An example I should follow?* Focus on spiritual lessons.

STEP 4: WHAT DOES GOD'S WORD MEAN IN MY LIFE?
(Listen to His Voice.)

Although this step will be the most meaningful for you, you can't do it effectively until you complete the first three steps. So, first rephrase the lessons you found in Step 3 and put them in the form of questions you could ask yourself, your spouse, your child, your friend, your neighbor, or your coworker. As you write the questions, listen for God to speak to you through His Word.

Be aware that there are some challenging passages in this study. Don't get hung up on what you don't understand, but just look for the *general principles* and *lessons* that can be learned. The introduction prior to the passages you will study in sessions 2–8, as well as the examples offered in Steps 2, 3, and 4 of this session, will help you get started.

Remember not to rush this process. It may take you several moments of prayerful meditation to discover meaningful lessons from the Scripture you are reading and hear God speaking to you. The object is not to "get through it" but to develop your personal relationship with God in order to grow in faith and learn to hear the whispers of the Holy Spirit.

STEP 5: LIVE IN OBEDIENT RESPONSE TO GOD'S WORD
(What will you do about what God has said?)

Read the assigned Scripture passages prayerfully, objectively, thoughtfully, and attentively as you listen for God to speak. Note that He may not speak to you through *every* verse, but He *will* speak. When He does, record the verse number (if applicable), what it is that God seems to be saying to you, and your response to Him. You might like to date these pages as a means not only of keeping a spiritual journal but also of holding yourself accountable to follow through in obedience. (See pages 6–7 for the example that Anne demonstrates in the video.) Afterward, it is your turn to try this method on your own using John 14:15–20. (See pages 8–9.)

STEP 1
Read God's Word
(Look at the Passage.)

STEP 2
What Does God's Word Say?
(List the Facts.)

Colossians 1:26–27

- **Reread God's Word**
- **List the outstanding facts with verse numbers**
- **Do not paraphrase**

26 the mystery that has been kept hidden for ages and generations, but is now disclosed to the saints.

v. 26 the mystery kept hidden for ages

v. 26 but now disclosed

27 To them God has chosen to make known among the Gentiles the glorious riches of this mystery, which is Christ in you, the hope of glory.

v. 27 God has chosen to make known this mystery

v. 27 which is Christ in you
v. 27 the hope of glory.

STEP 3
What Does God's Word Mean?
(Learn the Lessons.)

- **Write one spiritual lesson for each fact in Step 2.**
- **Is there an example to follow, a lesson to learn, a command to obey, a warning to heed, a promise to claim?**

v. 26 God does not always tell us everything.
The indwelling of the Holy Spirit was a mystery to Old Testament Saints.

v. 26 There comes a time when God does reveal to us an understanding of the truth.
The indwelling of the Holy Spirit is no longer a mystery, but a truth to be understood.

v. 27 Now is the time to grow in our understanding of that which we have not understood before.

v. 27 The mystery that Old Testament saints didn't know, and many people today do not understand, is that Jesus is available to dwell in us, in the Person of the Holy Spirit.

v. 27 Our confidence is that the Holy Spirit in us will conform us into the image of Jesus—that we will bring Him glory through our conduct and our character.

STEP 4
What Does God's Word Mean in My Life?
(Listen to His Voice.)

- **Put the lessons from Step 3 in the form of a question to ask yourself or someone else.**

v. 26 What have I not understood before now? Especially about the Holy Spirit?

v. 26 Is this the time when God will reveal to me a greater understanding of the truth about the Holy Spirit?

v. 27 Am I willing to use this study as a means to grow in my understanding of the Holy Spirit?

v. 27 What difference has it made in my life to understand that the Holy Spirit is Jesus in me?

v. 27 What has made me feel hopeless about myself? Why do I lack confidence that increasingly others will see Jesus in me? Is it because I am relying on myself for the transformation instead of the Holy Spirit?

STEP 5: Live in Obedient Response to God's Word   *Date:* _____
(What will you do about what God has said?)

I choose to use this study as a means to grow in my understanding of the Holy Spirit, who is Jesus in me; to share this mystery with others; and to live with confident dependence upon the Holy Spirit to change me from glory to glory until others see Jesus in me.

STEP 1
Read God's Word
(Look at the Passage.)

STEP 2
What Does God's Word Say?
(List the Facts.)

John 14:15–20

- Reread God's Word
- List the outstanding facts
  with verse numbers
- Do not paraphrase

15 "If you love me, you will obey what
  I command.

v. 15

16 And I will ask the Father, and he will
  give you another Counselor to be with
  you forever—

v. 16

17 the Spirit of truth. The world cannot
  accept him, because it neither sees him
  nor knows him. But you know him,
  for he lives with you and will be in you.

v. 17

18 I will not leave you as orphans; I will
  come to you.

v. 18

19 Before long, the world will not see
  me anymore, but you will see me.
  Because I live, you also will live.

v. 19

20 On that day you will realize that I am
  in my Father, and you are in me, and
  I am in you."

v. 20

STEP 3
What Does God's Word Mean?
(Learn the Lessons.)

- **Write one spiritual lesson for each fact in Step 2.**
- **Is there an example to follow, a lesson to learn, a command to obey, a warning to heed, a promise to claim?**

v. 15

v. 16

v. 17

v. 18

v. 19

v. 20

STEP 4
What Does God's Word Mean in My Life?
(Listen to His Voice.)

- **Put the lessons from Step 3 in the form of a question to ask yourself or someone else.**

v. 15 Whom should I obey

v. 16 Whom will the father send

v. 17 Who will reveal the truth about God to me

v. 18 Who will he w/me

v. 19 Who will reveal the truth to me.

v. 20 Do I understand the access I have to the father?

STEP 5: Live in Obedient Response to God's Word   *Date: _____*
(What will you do about what God has said?)

LOVING THE *Person* OF THE HOLY SPIRIT

One of my deepest, richest joys has been discovering by experience who the Holy Spirit is in every step of my life's journey.

—Anne Graham Lotz, *Jesus in Me*, page 9

WEEKLY SCHEDULE

DAY 1   3-Question Study—John 14:21–24

DAY 2   3-Question Study—John 14:25–27

DAY 3   3-Question Study—John 16:5–7

DAY 4   3-Question Study—Romans 8:9–11

DAY 5   3-Question Study—Romans 8:12–17

DAY 6   Reflection, Video Teaching, Group Discussion

Loving the *Person* of the Holy Spirit

Though you have not seen him, you love him.

—1 Peter 1:8

INDIVIDUAL STUDY INTRODUCTION

I'VE HEARD THE HOLY SPIRIT SPOKEN OF as an "it," a feeling, a dove, a flame of fire, a ghost, an emotion, or even an ecstatic experience. He is referred to as the third Person of the Trinity, as though He is the least of the Trinity, or a postscript to the more significant Father and Son. All of which is inaccurate.

While the Holy Spirit may be symbolized by a dove or flame of fire, while His presence may be accompanied by an emotion or feeling or ecstatic experience, He Himself is distinctly separate from those things. The Holy Spirit is not a thing but a Person.

So at the outset of our exploration of who the Holy Spirit is, keep in mind that He is a living Person who has a mind, a will, and emotions. He is referred to as the third Person of the Trinity not because He is the least, but because He is the third Person to be more fully revealed in Scripture. I can't wait for you to get to know Him better . . .

STEP 1
Read God's Word
(Look at the Passage.)

STEP 2
What Does God's Word Say?
(List the Facts.)

John 14:21–24

21 Whoever has my commands and keeps
them is the one who loves me. The one who
loves me will be loved by my Father, and I too
will love them and show myself to them.

22 Then Judas (not Judas Iscariot) said, "But, Lord,
why do you intend to show yourself to us
and not to the world?"

23 Jesus replied, "Anyone who loves me will obey
my teaching. My Father will love them, and we
will come to them and make our home with them.

24 Anyone who does not love me will not obey my
teaching. These words you hear are not my own;
they belong to the Father who sent me.

STEP 3
What Does God's
Word Mean?
(Learn the Lessons.)

STEP 4
What Does God's Word
Mean in My Life?
(Listen to His Voice.)

STEP 5: Live in Obedient Response to God's Word   *Date:* _____
(What will you do about what God has said?)

STEP 1	**STEP 2**
Read God's Word	What Does God's Word Say?
(Look at the Passage.)	*(List the Facts.)*

John 14:25–27

25 All this I have spoken while still with you.

26 But the Advocate, the Holy Spirit, whom the Father will send in my name, will teach you all things and will remind you of everything I have said to you.

27 Peace I leave with you; my peace I give you. I do not give to you as the world gives. Do not let your hearts be troubled and do not be afraid.

STEP 3
What Does God's
Word Mean?
(Learn the Lessons.)

STEP 4
What Does God's Word
Mean in My Life?
(Listen to His Voice.)

SESSION 2

STEP 5: Live in Obedient Response to God's Word   *Date:* _____
(What will you do about what God has said?)

STEP 1
Read God's Word
(Look at the Passage.)

STEP 2
What Does God's Word Say?
(List the Facts.)

John 16:5–7

5 But now I am going to him who sent me.
None of you asks me, 'Where are you
going?'

6 Rather, you are filled with grief because
I have said these things.

7 But very truly I tell you, it is for your good that
I am going away. Unless I go away, the Advocate
will not come to you; but if I go, I will send him
to you.

STEP 3
What Does God's Word Mean?
(Learn the Lessons.)

STEP 4
What Does God's Word Mean in My Life?
(Listen to His Voice.)

STEP 5: Live in Obedient Response to God's Word   *Date:* _____
(What will you do about what God has said?)

STEP 1
Read God's Word
(Look at the Passage.)

STEP 2
What Does God's Word Say?
(List the Facts.)

Romans 8:9–11

9 You, however, are not in the realm of the flesh, but are in the realm of the Spirit, if indeed the Spirit of God lives in you. And if anyone does not have the Spirit of Christ, they do not belong to Christ.

10 But if Christ is in you, then even though your body is subject to death because of sin, the Spirit gives life because of righteousness.

11 And if the Spirit of him who raised Jesus from the dead is living in you, he who raised Christ from the dead will also give life to your mortal bodies because of his Spirit who lives in you.

STEP 3
What Does God's
Word Mean?
(Learn the Lessons.)

STEP 4
What Does God's Word
Mean in My Life?
(Listen to His Voice.)

STEP 5: Live in Obedient Response to God's Word   *Date:* _____
(What will you do about what God has said?)

STEP 1
Read God's Word
(Look at the Passage.)

STEP 2
What Does God's Word Say?
(List the Facts.)

Romans 8:12–17

12 Therefore, brothers and sisters, we have
an obligation—but it is not to the flesh,
to live according to it.

13 For if you live according to the flesh you
will die; but if by the Spirit you put to death
the misdeeds of the body, you will live.

14 For those who are led by the Spirit of God
are the children of God.

15 The Spirit you received does not make you
slaves, so that you live in fear again; rather, the
Spirit you received brought about your adoption
to sonship. And by him we cry, "*Abba*, Father."

16 The Spirit himself testifies with our spirit,
that we are God's children.

17 Now if we are children, then we are heirs—
heirs of God and co-heirs with Christ, if indeed
we share in his sufferings in order that we may also
share in his glory.

STEP 3
What Does God's
Word Mean?
(Learn the Lessons.)

STEP 4
What Does God's Word
Mean in My Life?
(Listen to His Voice.)

STEP 5: Live in Obedient Response to God's Word   *Date:* _____
(What will you do about what God has said?)

REFLECTION

Record and journal the following from your study this week about the *Person* of the Holy Spirit.

The Scripture that stood out to you:

The lesson that stood out to you:

The one Live in Obedient Response to God's Word that you committed to this week:

HAVEN
TodAy

MATAN (GIFT) H/S

One thing I know for certain:

The Holy Spirit is not an

optional *extra* in my Christian life.

He is a *divine necessity.*

—Anne Graham Lotz,
Jesus in Me, page 3

GROUP STUDY

Welcome to session 2 of the *Jesus in Me* study!

NOTE: You just completed your first week of individual Bible study. If the 3-question study technique was new to your group, consider taking a few moments sharing thoughts on the experience before you dive into this week's video teaching. If anyone has questions or concerns about the individual study time, it is likely someone else feels the same way. Spend the time now to find resolution and answers together, so the remainder of this study can be productive and fruitful for everyone.

My prayer for you as we go through this study is that God Himself will draw near to you and you will experience the constant companionship of the Holy Spirit in a fresh new way. And as a result, you will come to love Him even more.

As we begin, let's open our Bibles and listen for the gentle whispers of the Holy Spirit. The Holy Spirit is wonderful. He is our Helper. He is our Comforter. He is our Counselor. He is our Strengthener. Our Standby. Our Advocate. Our Intercessor. He is another Jesus . . . Jesus living in us.

This week we begin our study by exploring the PERSON of the Holy Spirit.

WATCH VIDEO SESSION 2 (18 MINUTES)

SCRIPTURE IN THIS SESSION:
John 14:2–3, 5–6, 16, John 15:5, 18,
John 16:5–8, 12–16, Numbers 6:24–26, 2 Corinthians 1:4

Use this space to take notes if you like:

GROUP DISCUSSION QUESTIONS

1. What is something in the video teaching that either was striking or new to you?

2. Refer to your individual Bible studies this past week. What was one of the most significant lessons you recorded related to the Holy Spirit as a Person and why was it significant? To which verse did it relate?

3. How does the truth that the Holy Spirit is a Person change your perception of Him? Why do you think it is important to know the Holy Spirit as a living, thinking, feeling Person?

4. We heard multiple names by which the Holy Spirit is referred to in Scripture. Which of His names is most meaningful to you and why?

SESSION 2

WRAP UP

CLOSING PRAYER: Facilitator, pray over your group.

MOVING FORWARD: Review the next week's schedule on the page 32.

BLESSING & ENCOURAGEMENT: Finally, close your group meeting by reading the following blessing and encouragement over them before dismissing.

May your heart and mind be softened to the
Person of the Holy Spirit so that he can
"Teach you and remind you of everything Jesus said."
—JOHN 14:26

GOING DEEPER

To continue your study of the PERSON OF THE HOLY SPIRIT, read *Jesus in Me: Experiencing the Holy Spirit as a Constant Companion*, Part 1 (pages 5–44).

ENJOYING THE *Presence* OF THE HOLY SPIRIT

As an eternal Person, the Spirit of God has always been present
for all time and in all places. In fact, there is no place in the entire universe
where He has not, is not, or will not always be fully present. (Psalm 139:7)

—Anne Graham Lotz, *Jesus in Me*, page 53

WEEKLY SCHEDULE

DAY 1   3-Question Study—Genesis 1:1–3

DAY 2   3-Question Study—Acts 1:4–8

DAY 3   3-Question Study—Acts 2:1–8

DAY 4   3-Question Study—Acts 2:14–18

DAY 5   3-Question Study—Acts 2:36–39

DAY 6   Reflection, Video Teaching, Group Discussion

Enjoying the *Presence* of the Holy Spirit

You will fill me with joy in your presence.

—PSALM 16:11

INDIVIDUAL STUDY INTRODUCTION

How many things have been around us for a long time that we simply have not noticed? Like the bagel lever on my toaster. I recently went online to find another toaster because the one I've had for about twenty years no longer toasted both sides of the bread I put into it. When reading the reviews of the brand I was interested in, I came across one purchaser who was pleased that the model she selected toasted one side of her bagel while leaving the other side warm and chewy. I jumped up to see if that could be why my toaster was only toasting half of my bread slices. Sure enough. My toaster had a bagel feature that was turned on. When I turned it off and put in a slice of bread, both sides toasted evenly. I had to laugh, even as I felt foolish for not having noticed the bagel feature that had been there as long as I had owned the toaster.

While toasters are nowhere near the significance of the Holy Spirit, could it be for many of us that we also have never really noticed Him either? Maybe we've never been taught to notice Him. This week we are going to focus in on His presence. Right here. Right now.

STEP 1
Read God's Word
(Look at the Passage.)

STEP 2
What Does God's Word Say?
(List the Facts.)

Genesis 1:1–3

1 In the beginning God created the heavens and the earth.

2 Now the earth was formless and empty, darkness was over the surface of the deep, and the Spirit of God was hovering over the waters.

3 And God said, "Let there be light," and there was light.

STEP 3
What Does God's Word Mean?
(Learn the Lessons.)

STEP 4
What Does God's Word Mean in My Life?
(Listen to His Voice.)

STEP 5: Live in Obedient Response to God's Word   *Date:* _____
(What will you do about what God has said?)

STEP 1
Read God's Word
(Look at the Passage.)

STEP 2
What Does God's Word Say?
(List the Facts.)

Acts 1:4–8

4 On one occasion, while he [Jesus] was eating with them, he gave them this command: "Do not leave Jerusalem, but wait for the gift my Father promised, which you have heard me speak about.

5 For John baptized with water, but in a few days you will be baptized with the Holy Spirit."

6 Then they gathered around him and asked him, "Lord, are you at this time going to restore the kingdom to Israel?"

7 He said to them: "It is not for you to know the times or dates the Father has set by his own authority.

8 But you will receive power when the Holy Spirit comes on you; and you will be my witnesses in Jerusalem, and in all Judea and Samaria, and to the ends of the earth."

STEP 3
What Does God's
Word Mean?
(Learn the Lessons.)

STEP 4
What Does God's Word
Mean in My Life?
(Listen to His Voice.)

STEP 5: Live in Obedient Response to God's Word   *Date:* _____
(What will you do about what God has said?)

STEP 1
Read God's Word
(Look at the Passage.)

STEP 2
What Does God's Word Say?
(List the Facts.)

Acts 2:1–8

1 When the day of Pentecost came, they were all together in one place.

2 Suddenly a sound like the blowing of a violent wind came from heaven and filled the whole house where they were sitting.

3 They saw what seemed to be tongues of fire that separated and came to rest on each of them.

4 All of them were filled with the Holy Spirit and began to speak in other tongues as the Spirit enabled them.

5 Now there were staying in Jerusalem God-fearing Jews from every nation under heaven.

6 When they heard this sound, a crowd came together in bewilderment, because each one heard their own language being spoken.

7 Utterly amazed, they asked: "Aren't all these who are speaking Galileans?

8 Then how is it that each of us hears them in our native language?"

STEP 3
What Does God's
Word Mean?
(Learn the Lessons.)

STEP 4
What Does God's Word
Mean in My Life?
(Listen to His Voice.)

STEP 5: Live in Obedient Response to God's Word   *Date:* _____
(What will you do about what God has said?)

STEP 1
Read God's Word
(Look at the Passage.)

Acts 2:14–18

14 Then Peter stood up with the Eleven,
raised his voice and addressed the
crowd: "Fellow Jews and all of you who
live in Jerusalem, let me explain this
to you; listen carefully to what I say.

15 These people are not drunk, as you suppose.
It's only nine in the morning!

16 No, this is what was spoken by the prophet Joel:

17 In the last days, God says, "I will pour out my
Spirit on all people. Your sons and daughters
will prophesy, your young men will see visions,
your old men will dream dreams.

18 Even on my servants, both men and women,
I will pour out my Spirit in those days, and
they will prophesy."

STEP 2
What Does God's Word Say?
(List the Facts.)

STEP 3
What Does God's Word Mean?
(Learn the Lessons.)

STEP 4
What Does God's Word Mean in My Life?
(Listen to His Voice.)

SESSION 3

STEP 5: Live in Obedient Response to God's Word   *Date:* _____
(What will you do about what God has said?)

STEP 1
Read God's Word
(Look at the Passage.)

STEP 2
What Does God's Word Say?
(List the Facts.)

Acts 2:36–39

36 "Therefore let all Israel be assured of this; God has made this Jesus, whom you crucified, both Lord and Messiah."

37 When the people heard this, they were cut to the heart and said to Peter and the other apostles, "Brothers, what shall we do?"

38 Peter replied, "Repent and be baptized, every one of you, in the name of Jesus Christ for the forgiveness of your sins. And you will receive the gift of the Holy Spirit.

39 The promise is for you and your children and for all who are far off—for all whom the Lord our God will call."

STEP 3
What Does God's
Word Mean?
(Learn the Lessons.)

STEP 4
What Does God's Word
Mean in My Life?
(Listen to His Voice.)

STEP 5: Live in Obedient Response to God's Word   *Date:* _____
(What will you do about what God has said?)

REFLECTION

Record and journal the following from your study this week about the PRESENCE of the Holy Spirit.

The Scripture that stood out to you:

The lesson that stood out to you:

The one Live in Obedient Response to God's Word that you committed to this week:

Do you long for faith that really works? Then fully

embrace the Holy Spirit with absolute, total,

unreserved trust, and begin experiencing

His constant presence . . . on the inside.

—Anne Graham Lotz,
Jesus in Me, page 76

GROUP STUDY

Welcome to session 3 of the *Jesus in Me* Bible study!

We continue our study this week exploring the PRESENCE of the Holy Spirit.

Some of us may have made some profound discoveries this week in our individual Bible study time. Some of us may have come to an awareness of the presence of the Holy Spirit we did not previously have. Each of us is on a beautiful journey with the Lord in this study. It is a blessing to share this experience together openly and honestly. Hearing from each other can open our own ears to what the Spirit may be further saying to us!

WATCH VIDEO SESSION 3 (17:30 MINUTES)

SCRIPTURE IN THIS SESSION:
Genesis 1:1–3, John 16:7, Acts 2:6, 1 Samuel 9, Psalm 51:11, Hebrews 13:5, John 14:17

SESSION 3

Use this space to take notes if you like:

If you've just prayed with Anne, we'd love to hear from you! Drop us a note at angelmin.info@angelministries.org.

GROUP DISCUSSION QUESTIONS

1. Open your group discussion by sharing something in the video teaching that either was striking or new to you.

2. Refer to your individual Bible studies this past week. What was one of the most significant lessons you recorded related to the presence of the Holy Spirit and why was it significant? To which verse did it relate?

3. What difference did the Holy Spirit make at Creation? Do you think His power is less today?

4. What is most significant to you about the difference between the Old Testament experience of the Holy Spirit and the New Testament experience after Jesus sent Him?

SESSION 3

WRAP UP

CLOSING PRAYER: Facilitator, pray over your group.

MOVING FORWARD: Review the next week's schedule on page 52.

BLESSING & ENCOURAGEMENT: Finally, close your group meeting by reading the following blessing and encouragement over them before dismissing.

May you experience a fresh filling of the Holy Spirit this week.
May you be full of worship and
enjoyment and adoration for the One
who was present in the beginning
and has come to live and dwell in you.

GOING DEEPER

To continue your study of THE PRESENCE OF THE HOLY SPIRIT, read *Jesus in Me: Experiencing the Holy Spirit as a Constant Companion*, Part 2 (pages 45–76).

RELYING ON THE *Power*
OF THE HOLY SPIRIT

While you have the power of the Holy Spirit within you,
the cooperation of your full surrender, obedience, and faith is required to activate it.

—Anne Graham Lotz, *Jesus in Me*, page 91

WEEKLY SCHEDULE

DAY 1   3-Question Study—Acts 3:1–7

DAY 2   3-Question Study—Acts 4:1–4

DAY 3   3-Question Study—Acts 4:5–13

DAY 4   3-Question Study—Ephesians 3:16–19

DAY 5   3-Question Study—Ephesians 1:15–21

DAY 6   Reflection, Video Teaching, Group Discussion

Relying on the *Power* of the Holy Spirit

"But you will receive power when the Holy Spirit comes on you; and you will be my witness in Jerusalem, and in all Judea and Samaria, and to the ends of the earth."

—Acts 1:8

INDIVIDUAL STUDY INTRODUCTION

ALTHOUGH YOU HAVE ENTERED INTO A PERSONAL RELATIONSHIP with God through faith in Jesus, do you find yourself from time to time running on empty? Are you trying harder to be a "good Christian," putting more and more effort into pleasing God, only to find the desired result elusive? Do you find yourself just going through the motions? Are you attending church and even this Bible study, but increasingly you're living behind a facade, pretending to be more spiritual than you really are? With a fake smile on your lips and the "proper" words on your tongue, are you just trying to make it one more week . . . one more day . . . one more hour . . . one more step? Hoping against hope no one notices, because surely no one else is experiencing this struggle. Is your mind gripped by the thought, "I can't do this? I'm just not cut out to live the Christian life."

Don't be discouraged. There is hope! The One who is within you will enable you to live out the commitment you have made. The key is learning to rely on His power, which is the subject of our study this week.

STEP 1
Read God's Word
(Look at the Passage.)

STEP 2
What Does God's Word Say?
(List the Facts.)

Acts 3:1–7

1 One day Peter and John were going up to
the temple at the time of prayer—at three
in the afternoon.

2 Now a man who was lame from birth was
being carried to the temple gate called
Beautiful, where he was put every day to
beg from those going into the temple courts.

3 When he saw Peter and John about to enter,
he asked them for money.

4 Peter looked straight at him, as did John.
Then Peter said, "Look at us!"

5 So the man gave them his attention, expecting
to get something from them.

6 Then Peter said, "Silver or gold I do not have,
but what I do have I give you. In the name of
Jesus Christ of Nazareth walk."

7 Taking him by the right hand, he helped him up,
and instantly the man's feet and ankles became strong.

STEP 3
What Does God's
Word Mean?
(Learn the Lessons.)

STEP 4
What Does God's Word
Mean in My Life?
(Listen to His Voice.)

Jn   3:16

Tim   3 - 18

STEP 5: Live in Obedient Response to God's Word   *Date:* _____
(What will you do about what God has said?)

STEP 1
Read God's Word
(Look at the Passage.)

STEP 2
What Does God's Word Say?
(List the Facts.)

Acts 4:1–4

1 The priests and the captain of the temple guard and the Sadducees came up to Peter and John while they were speaking to the people.

2 They were greatly disturbed because the apostles were teaching the people, proclaiming in Jesus the resurrection of the dead.

3 They seized Peter and John and, because it was evening, they put them in jail until the next day.

4 But many who heard the message believed; so the number of men who believed grew to about five thousand.

STEP 3
What Does God's
Word Mean?
(Learn the Lessons.)

STEP 4
What Does God's Word
Mean in My Life?
(Listen to His Voice.)

STEP 5: Live in Obedient Response to God's Word　　*Date:* _____
(What will you do about what God has said?)

STEP 1	**STEP 2**
Read God's Word	What Does God's Word Say?
(Look at the Passage.)	*(List the Facts.)*

Acts 4:5–13

5 The next day the rulers, the elders and the teachers of the law met in Jerusalem.

6 Annas the high priest was there, and so were Caiaphas, John, Alexander and others of the high priest's family.

7 They had Peter and John brought before them and began to question them: "By what power or what name did you do this?"

8 Then Peter, filled with the Holy Spirit, said to them: "Rulers and elders of the people!

9 If we are being called to account today for an act of kindness shown to a man who was lame and are being asked how he was healed,

10 then know this, you and all the people of Israel: It is by the name of Jesus Christ of Nazareth, whom you crucified but whom God raised from the dead, that this man stands before you healed.

11 Jesus is " 'the stone you builders rejected, which has become the cornerstone.'

12 Salvation is found in no one else, for there is no other name under heaven given to mankind by which we must be saved."

13 When they saw the courage of Peter and John and realized that they were unschooled, ordinary men, they were astonished and they took note that these men had been with Jesus.

STEP 3
What Does God's
Word Mean?
(Learn the Lessons.)

STEP 4
What Does God's Word
Mean in My Life?
(Listen to His Voice.)

STEP 5: Live in Obedient Response to God's Word   *Date:* _____

(What will you do about what God has said?)

STEP 1
Read God's Word
(Look at the Passage.)

STEP 2
What Does God's Word Say?
(List the Facts.)

Ephesians 3:16–19

16 I pray that out of his glorious riches
he may strengthen you with power
through his Spirit in your inner being,

17 So that Christ may dwell in your hearts
through faith. And I pray that you, being
rooted and established in love,

18 may have power, together with all the Lord's
holy people, to grasp how wide and long and
high and deep is the love of Christ,

19 and to know this love that surpasses knowledge—
that you may be filled to the measure of all the
fullness of God.

STEP 3
What Does God's
Word Mean?
(Learn the Lessons.)

STEP 4
What Does God's Word
Mean in My Life?
(Listen to His Voice.)

SESSION 4

STEP 5: Live in Obedient Response to God's Word   *Date:* _____
(What will you do about what God has said?)

STEP 1
Read God's Word
(Look at the Passage.)

STEP 2
What Does God's Word Say?
(List the Facts.)

Ephesians 1:15–21

15 For this reason, ever since I heard about
your faith in the Lord Jesus and your love
for all God's people,

16 I have not stopped giving thanks for you,
remembering you in my prayers.

17 I keep asking that the God of our Lord Jesus
Christ, the glorious Father, may give you the
Spirit of wisdom and revelation, so that you may
know him better.

18 I pray that the eyes of your heart may be
enlightened in order that you may know the hope
to which he has called you, the riches of his glorious
inheritance in his holy people,

19 and his incomparably great power for us who believe.
That power is the same as the mighty strength

20 which he exerted in Christ when he raised him from
the dead and seated him at his right hand in the
heavenly realms

21 far above all rule and authority, power and dominion,
and every name that is invoked, not only in the present
age but also in the one to come.

STEP 3
What Does God's
Word Mean?
(Learn the Lessons.)

STEP 4
What Does God's Word
Mean in My Life?
(Listen to His Voice.)

STEP 5: Live in Obedient Response to God's Word   *Date:* _____
(What will you do about what God has said?)

REFLECTION

Record and journal the following from your study this week about the POWER of the Holy Spirit.

The Scripture that stood out to you:

The lesson that stood out to you:

The one Live in Obedient Response to God's Word that you committed to this week:

When you restrict His access in your life,

you give up being filled with the Spirit

and you deny yourself access to

all His spiritual blessings,

including His power and

eternal purpose for your life.

—Anne Graham Lotz, *Jesus in Me*, page 251

GROUP STUDY

Welcome to session 4 of the *Jesus in Me* Bible study!

This week we have been learning about relying on the POWER of the Holy Spirit and what that power is meant for and how we can better understand it. In today's teaching, Anne will dig into what is required of us practically in order to receive and experience and even wield the power of the Holy Spirit. As we get deeper into this study and explore topics that may still be new to some, may be uncomfortable for others, or may be exhilarating and exciting for yet others, let's commit ourselves to building one another up as Scripture encourages us to do (1 Thessalonians 5:11; Hebrews 3:13; Jude 1:20).

WATCH VIDEO SESSION 4 (17 MINUTES)

SCRIPTURE IN THIS SESSION:
Genesis 1, Ephesians 5:18, 2 Corinthians 3:18,
Acts 2:14–40, Acts 2:37–38, John 16:8–11

Use this space to take notes if you like:

GROUP DISCUSSION QUESTIONS

1. Open your group discussion by sharing something in the video teaching that either was striking or new to you.

2. Refer to your individual Bible studies this past week. What was one of the most significant lessons you recorded related to the power or transformation given by the Holy Spirit, and why was it significant? To which verse did it relate?

3. Discuss how the Holy Spirit can change someone. How does this impact the way you pray for others? How does this encourage you when you share the gospel?

4. What evidence of the Holy Spirit's filling should others be able to see in your life? Discuss how you can develop in these ways. What would help you to better reflect Jesus?

WRAP UP

CLOSING PRAYER: Facilitator, pray over your group.

MOVING FORWARD: Review the next week's schedule on page 72.

BLESSING & ENCOURAGEMENT: Finally, close your group meeting by reading the following blessing and encouragement over them before dismissing.

He gives strength to the weary

and increases the power of the weak.

Even youths grow tired and weary,

and young men stumble and fall;

But those who hope in the LORD

will renew their strength.

—ISAIAH 40:29–31 (NIV)

GOING DEEPER

To continue your study of THE POWER OF THE HOLY SPIRIT, read *Jesus in Me: Experiencing the Holy Spirit as a Constant Companion*, Part 3 (pages 77–110).

SESSION 4

EMBRACING THE *Purpose* OF THE HOLY SPIRIT

In some ways, our lives are like a symphony. And the Holy Spirit is the conductor. He is the one who brings forth the beautiful music of a life that glorifies God.

—Anne Graham Lotz, *Jesus in Me*, page 115

WEEKLY SCHEDULE

Day 1   3-Question Study—Matthew 26:31–35

Day 2   3-Question Study—Matthew 26:69–75

Day 3   3-Question Study—John 21:15–17

Day 4   3-Question Study—Ephesians 2:1–5

Day 5   3-Question Study—Hebrews 10:19–25

Day 6   Reflection, Video Teaching, Group Discussion

Embracing the *Purpose* of the Holy Spirit

And we all, who with unveiled faces contemplate the Lord's glory, are being transformed into his image with ever-increasing glory, which comes from the Lord, who is the Spirit.
—2 Corinthians 3:18

INDIVIDUAL STUDY INTRODUCTION

Like me, have you sometimes thought of priorities in the same way you think of New Year's resolutions? A list might look something like this:

- Lose weight
- Start exercising
- Join a gym
- Get in shape
- Drink less Diet Coke
- Drink more water
- Eat less sugar
- Read a book
- Got to bed/get up earlier

Like using a shotgun to shoot a fly, hoping that at least one of the hundreds of bits of buckshot will hit it, we make resolutions hoping to keep at least one of them so we will be better off at the end of the year. The reality is that we rarely keep any of them for the next month, much less the next twelve months.

Sadly, many of us conduct our lives according to this same philosophy. We react to life's challenges and opportunities with no clearly defined purpose, which means we don't have clarity as to how to prioritize our days. In the end, we find ourselves with a life that is at best scattered like buckshot with few worthwhile things to show for it, or is at worst wasted and devoid of eternal significance.

Which is why we need to embrace the Purpose of the Holy Spirit.

STEP 1
Read God's Word
(Look at the Passage.)

Matthew 26:31–35

31 Then Jesus told them, "This very night you will all fall away on account of me, for it is written: 'I will strike the shepherd, and the sheep of the flock will be scattered.'

32 But after I have risen, I will go ahead of you into Galilee."

33 Peter replied, "Even if all fall away on account of you, I never will."

34 "Truly I tell you," Jesus answered, "this very night, before the rooster crows, you will disown me three times."

35 But Peter declared, "Even if I have to die with you, I will never disown you." And all the other disciples said the same.

STEP 2
What Does God's Word Say?
(List the Facts.)

STEP 3
What Does God's
Word Mean?
(Learn the Lessons.)

STEP 4
What Does God's Word
Mean in My Life?
(Listen to His Voice.)

STEP 5: Live in Obedient Response to God's Word   *Date:* _____
(What will you do about what God has said?)

STEP 1
Read God's Word
(Look at the Passage.)

STEP 2
What Does God's Word Say?
(List the Facts.)

Matthew 26:69–75

69 Now Peter was sitting out in the courtyard, and a servant girl came to him. "You also were with Jesus of Galilee," she said.

70 But he denied it before them all. "I don't know what you're talking about," he said.

71 Then he went out to the gateway, where another servant girl saw him and said to the people there, "This fellow was with Jesus of Nazareth."

72 He denied it again, with an oath: "I don't know the man!"

73 After a little while, those standing there went up to Peter and said, "Surely you are one of them; your accent gives you away."

74 Then he began to call down curses, and he swore to them, "I don't know the man!" Immediately a rooster crowed.

75 Then Peter remembered the word Jesus had spoken: "Before the rooster crows, you will disown me three times." And he went outside and wept bitterly.

STEP 3
What Does God's
Word Mean?
(Learn the Lessons.)

STEP 4
What Does God's Word
Mean in My Life?
(Listen to His Voice.)

STEP 5: Live in Obedient Response to God's Word   *Date: _____*
(What will you do about what God has said?)

STEP 1
Read God's Word
(Look at the Passage.)

STEP 2
What Does God's Word Say?
(List the Facts.)

John 21:15–17

15 When they had finished eating, Jesus said to
Simon Peter, "Simon son of John, do you love
me more than these?" "Yes, Lord," he said,
"you know that I love you." Jesus said,
"Feed my lambs."

16 Again Jesus said, "Simon son of John, do you
love me?" He answered, "Yes, Lord, you know
that I love you." Jesus said, "Take care of my sheep."

17 The third time he said to him, "Simon son of John,
do you love me?" Peter was hurt because Jesus
asked him the third time, "Do you love me?"
He said, "Lord, you know all things; you know
that I love you." Jesus said, "Feed my sheep."

STEP 3
What Does God's
Word Mean?
(Learn the Lessons.)

STEP 4
What Does God's Word
Mean in My Life?
(Listen to His Voice.)

STEP 5: Live in Obedient Response to God's Word   *Date:* _____
(What will you do about what God has said?)

STEP 1
Read God's Word
(Look at the Passage.)

STEP 2
What Does God's Word Say?
(List the Facts.)

Ephesians 2:1–5

1 As for you, you were dead in your
transgressions and sins,

2 In which you used to live when you followed
the ways of this world and of the ruler of the
kingdom of the air, the spirit who is now at
work in those who are disobedient.

3 All of us also lived among them at one time,
gratifying the cravings of our flesh and
following its desires and thoughts. Like the rest,
we were by nature deserving of wrath.

4 But because of his great love for us, God,
who is rich in mercy,

5 made us alive with Christ even when we
were dead in transgressions—it is by grace
you have been saved.

STEP 3
What Does God's
Word Mean?
(Learn the Lessons.)

STEP 4
What Does God's Word
Mean in My Life?
(Listen to His Voice.)

STEP 5: Live in Obedient Response to God's Word   *Date:* _____
(What will you do about what God has said?)

STEP 1
Read God's Word
(Look at the Passage.)

STEP 2
What Does God's Word Say?
(List the Facts.)

Hebrews 10:19–25

19 Therefore, brothers and sisters, since we
have confidence to enter the Most Holy
Place by the blood of Jesus,

20 by a new and living way opened for us
through the curtain, that is, his body,

21 and since we have a great priest over the
house of God,

22 let us draw near to God with a sincere heart
and with the full assurance that faith brings,
having our hearts sprinkled to cleanse us
from a guilty conscience and having our
bodies washed with pure water.

23 Let us hold unswervingly to the hope we
profess, for he who promised is faithful.

24 And let us consider how we may spur one
another on toward love and good deeds,

25 not giving up meeting together, as some
are in the habit of doing, but encouraging
one another—and all the more as you see the
Day approaching.

STEP 3
What Does God's
Word Mean?
(Learn the Lessons.)

STEP 4
What Does God's Word
Mean in My Life?
(Listen to His Voice.)

STEP 5: Live in Obedient Response to God's Word   *Date:* _____
(What will you do about what God has said?)

REFLECTION

Record and journal the following from your study this week about the PURPOSE of the Holy Spirit.

The Scripture that stood out to you:

The lesson that stood out to you:

The one Live in Obedient Response to God's Word that you committed to this week:

Jesus promised that "He will guide you into all truth." So, ask Him to guide your focus until it's laser-like in steadfast resolution to bring God glory in all you say and do. Then relax. Regardless of whatever life may bring your way, embrace the Spirit's purpose.

—Anne Graham Lotz, *Jesus in Me*, page 129

GROUP STUDY

Welcome to session 5 of the *Jesus in Me* Bible study!

Does the purpose for which you have been living challenge you? Does it fulfill you? Or have you sensed a restless emptiness deep within? Have you longed to live for something more, bigger, or greater?

Where does that desire for something greater come from? Why are we stirred to yearn for a life that is more than ordinary? One reason is that we are created in the image of God with the capacity to know Him in a personal, permanent relationship for the purpose of bringing Him glory. Until that purpose is fulfilled, we will be empty, deeply dissatisfied and unfulfilled as we continually try to fill the void with substitutes.

But if you have established a personal relationship with God and you still feel unfulfilled and dissatisfied, it could be that the Holy Spirit is stirring you up, trying to direct your attention to your life's purpose.

This week we have transitioned from the "who" to the "for what", as we learn about the PURPOSE of the Holy Spirit.

WATCH VIDEO SESSION 5 (15 MINUTES)

<u>SCRIPTURE IN THIS SESSION:</u>
Genesis 12:1, 2 Chronicles 20:7, Isaiah 41:8,
James 2:23, Ephesians 1:6, 2:10, Genesis 50, Romans 8:28

Use this space to take notes if you like:

GROUP DISCUSSION QUESTIONS

1. Open your group discussion by sharing something in the video teaching that either was striking or new to you.

2. Refer to your individual Bible studies this past week. What was one of the most significant lessons you recorded related to the purpose of the Holy Spirit, and why was it significant? To which verse did it relate?

3. After being together for five sessions, what spiritual gifts do you see in each other? How can you use your spiritual gifts to build each other up?

Ministry Gifts

4. In what ways is your confidence in God strengthened more in times of comfort or in times of crisis? What conflict, chaos, and disruption could be part of God's purpose to strengthen your faith?

WRAP UP

CLOSING PRAYER: Facilitator, pray over your group.

MOVING FORWARD: Review the next week's schedule on page 92.

BLESSING & ENCOURAGEMENT: Finally, close your group meeting by reading the following blessing and encouragement over them before dismissing.

May the Holy Spirit guide you in steadfast resolution
to know God and embrace the Spirit's purpose
for you to glorify Him in all you say and in all you do.

GOING DEEPER

To continue your study of THE PURPOSE OF THE HOLY SPIRIT, read *Jesus in Me: Experiencing the Holy Spirit as a Constant Companion,* Part 4 (pages 111–148).

LIVING BY THE *Precepts* OF THE HOLY SPIRIT

*My love of reading, studying, applying, and obeying my Bible
has led me to the deep conviction that it is more than just great literature.
There is something supernatural about it. It works!*

—Anne Graham Lotz, *Jesus in Me*, page 153

WEEKLY SCHEDULE

DAY 1   3-Question Study—Matthew 4:1–4

DAY 2   3-Question Study—Matthew 4:5–11

DAY 3   3-Question Study—2 Timothy 3:14–17

DAY 4   3-Question Study—1 John 2:3–6

DAY 5   3-Question Study—Psalm 1

DAY 6   Reflection, Video Teaching, Group Discussion

Living by the *Precepts* of the Holy Spirit

All Scripture is God-breathed and is useful for teaching, rebuking,
correcting and training in righteousness . . .

—2 Timothy 3:16

INDIVIDUAL STUDY INTRODUCTION

WHILE I OWNED SOME CHILD-FRIENDLY VERSIONS of the Bible when growing up, my first "real" Bible was a navy, leather-bound, King James Version, Scofield edition. Mother and Daddy gave it to me at my baptism. It is a treasure that I still have safely on my bookshelf. In the flyleaf, my mother wrote these words:

"To Anne– (who on this January 13, 1957 publicly took her stand for Christ, her Savior), we give this Book, your one sure guide in an unsure world. Read it, study it, love it, live it. In it you will find a verse for every occasion. Hide them in your heart."

Although my mother's words were written over sixty years ago, their wisdom transcends generations, cultures, world events, time, and age.

My love of reading, studying, applying, and obeying my Bible has led me to the deep conviction that it is more than just great literature. There is something supernatural about it. It works! It pulsates with life! How could that be? What makes it so unique? The answer to those questions leads us straight to the Holy Spirit.

STEP 1
Read God's Word
(Look at the Passage.)

STEP 2
What Does God's Word Say?
(List the Facts.)

Matthew 4:1–4

1 Then Jesus was led by the Spirit into the wilderness to be tempted by the devil.

2 After fasting forty days and forty nights, he was hungry.

3 The tempter came to him and said, "If you are the Son of God, tell these stones to become bread."

4 Jesus answered, "It is written: 'Man shall not live on bread alone, but on every word that comes from the mouth of God.'"

STEP 3
What Does God's
Word Mean?
(Learn the Lessons.)

STEP 4
What Does God's Word
Mean in My Life?
(Listen to His Voice.)

I must balance my physical needs w/
spiritual things by study in the word of God
PP praying · being led #/B for guidance

STEP 5: Live in Obedient Response to God's Word   *Date:* _____
(What will you do about what God has said?)

STEP 1
Read God's Word
(Look at the Passage.)

STEP 2
What Does God's Word Say?
(List the Facts.)

Matthew 4:5–11

5 Then the devil took him to the holy city and had him stand on the highest point of the temple.

6 "If you are the Son of God," he said, "throw yourself down. For it is written: 'He will command his angels concerning you, and they will lift you up in their hands, so that you will not strike your foot against a stone.'"

7 Jesus answered him, "It is also written: 'Do not put the Lord your God to the test.'"

8 Again, the devil took him to a very high mountain and showed him all the kingdoms of the world and their splendor.

9 "All this I will give you," he said, "if you will bow down and worship me."

10 Jesus said to him, "Away from me, Satan! For it is written: 'Worship the Lord your God and serve him only.'"

11 Then the devil left him, and angels came and attended him.

STEP 3
What Does God's
Word Mean?
(Learn the Lessons.)

STEP 4
What Does God's Word
Mean in My Life?
(Listen to His Voice.)

If even Jesus was tempted by the Devil why do I think I could (would) not be tempted - Help me not give into temptation.

STEP 5: Live in Obedient Response to God's Word   *Date:* _____
(What will you do about what God has said?)

STEP 1
Read God's Word
(Look at the Passage.)

STEP 2
What Does God's Word Say?
(List the Facts.)

2 Timothy 3:14–17

14 But as for you, continue in what you have learned and have become convinced of, because you know those from whom you learned it,

15 and how from infancy you have known the Holy Scriptures, which are able to make you wise for salvation through faith in Christ Jesus.

16 All Scripture is God-breathed, and is useful for teaching, rebuking, correcting and training in righteousness,

17 so that the servant of God may be thoroughly equipped for every good work.

STEP 3
What Does God's
Word Mean?
(Learn the Lessons.)

STEP 4
What Does God's Word
Mean in My Life?
(Listen to His Voice.)

STEP 5: Live in Obedient Response to God's Word   *Date:* _____
(What will you do about what God has said?)

STEP 1
Read God's Word
(Look at the Passage.)

STEP 2
What Does God's Word Say?
(List the Facts.)

1 John 2:3–6

3 We know that we have come to know him if we keep his commands.

4 Whoever says, "I know him," but does not do what he commands is a liar, and the truth is not in that person.

5 But if anyone obeys his word, love for God is truly made complete in them. This is how we know we are in him.

6 Whoever claims to live in him must live as Jesus did.

STEP 3
What Does God's Word Mean?
(Learn the Lessons.)

STEP 4
What Does God's Word Mean in My Life?
(Listen to His Voice.)

STEP 5: Live in Obedient Response to God's Word   *Date:* _____
(What will you do about what God has said?)

STEP 1
Read God's Word
(Look at the Passage.)

STEP 2
What Does God's Word Say?
(List the Facts.)

Psalm 1:1–6

1 Blessed is the one who does not walk in step
with the wicked or stand in the way that
sinners take or sit in the company of mockers,

2 but whose delight is in the law of the LORD, and
who meditates on his law day and night.

3 That person is like a tree planted by streams of
water, which yields its fruit in season and whose
leaf does not wither—whatever they do prospers.

4 Not so the wicked! They are like chaff that
the wind blows away.

5 Therefore the wicked will not stand in the
judgment, nor sinners in the assembly of
the righteous.

6 For the LORD watches over the way of the
righteous, but the way of the wicked leads
to destruction.

STEP 3
What Does God's Word Mean?
(Learn the Lessons.)

STEP 4
What Does God's Word Mean in My Life?
(Listen to His Voice.)

STEP 5: Live in Obedient Response to God's Word   *Date: _____*
(What will you do about what God has said?)

REFLECTION

Record and journal the following from your study this week about the PRECEPTS of the Holy Spirit.

The Scripture that stood out to you:

The lesson that stood out to you:

The one Live in Obedient Response to God's Word that you committed to this week:

This exercise [of Bible study] is simple

but challenging in that it requires you and me to think

for ourselves. It effectively removes the "middleman"

and allows us to hear directly from the

Spirit through God's Word.

—Anne Graham Lotz, *Jesus in Me*, page 246

GROUP STUDY

Welcome to session 6 of the Jesus in Me Bible study!

All Scripture from Genesis to Revelation is God-breathed because it is inspired by the Holy Spirit—the Spirit of Truth. So regardless of the way you were raised, what is your opinion of the Bible now and how was that opinion formed? Have you been influenced by others who are critical? Have you been taught that it is a good book that contains God's Word, but it is not God's Word in its entirety? Have you been told that the Bible contains errors or myths?

Whatever your opinion about the Bible has been up until this moment, I want to challenge you to decide now, once and for all, that you believe it. Why? *Because it is God's Word. It is backed by His character.*

Read it and live it out for yourself. You will discover the same thing that I discovered. The Bible works. Then choose to place your faith in the Bible as being true, inspired, and infallible. Follow the Creator's directions for life. Live by the precepts of the Holy Spirit.

We praise God that you are persevering and endeavoring to experience the Holy Spirit as a constant companion!

WATCH VIDEO SESSION 6 (16:30 MINUTES)

SCRIPTURE IN THIS SESSION:
John 16:13, 2 Timothy 3:16, Revelation 19,
Jeremiah 36:4, 16–24, 27–39,
Genesis 3:1, Matthew 5:18, 2 Kings 5

Use this space to take notes if you like:

GROUP DISCUSSION QUESTIONS

1. Open your group discussion by sharing something in the video teaching that either was striking or new to you.

2. Refer to your individual Bible studies this past week. What was one of the most significant lessons you recorded on the precepts of the Holy Spirit, and why was it significant? To which verse did it relate?

3. In order to live by God's precepts and follow His directions for living, we must read them. How do you structure your daily time in God's Word? Share any helpful ideas with the group.

4. Make a list of practical steps you will take today to start following God's directions more closely. Consider challenges and obstacles and outright opposition you may encounter. How can you be prepared to follow through?

WRAP UP

CLOSING PRAYER: Facilitator, pray over your group.

MOVING FORWARD: Review the next week's schedule on page 112.

BLESSING & ENCOURAGEMENT: Finally, close your group meeting by reading the following blessing and encouragement over them before dismissing.

May you receive and trust the Word of Jesus:

"But when He, the Spirit of Truth comes,

He will guide you into all truth."

—JOHN 16:13

GOING DEEPER

To continue your study of THE PRECEPTS OF THE HOLY SPIRIT, read *Jesus in Me: Experiencing the Holy Spirit as a Constant Companion*, Part 5 (pages 149–166).

REFLECTING THE *Purity*
OF THE HOLY SPIRIT

I believe the church today is in desperate need of revival. Authentic revival.
Not a tent meeting or a series of services to save the lost, but a spiritual awakening that will
compel God's people to repent of our sin, return to the cross,
and recommit ourselves to living lives that reflect His purity.

—Anne Graham Lotz, *Jesus in Me*, page 174

WEEKLY SCHEDULE

DAY 1   3-Question Study—Acts 5:1–6

DAY 2   3-Question Study—Acts 5:7–11

DAY 3   3-Question Study—1 John 1:5–10

DAY 4   3-Question Study—Philippians 1:9–11

DAY 5   3-Question Study—1 Peter 1:13–16

DAY 6   Reflection, Video Teaching, Group Discussion

Reflecting the *Purity* of the Holy Spirit

Set an example for the believers in speech, in life, in love, in faith and in purity.
—1 Timothy 4:12

INDIVIDUAL STUDY INTRODUCTION

You and I live surrounded by a culture that has become spiritually and morally bankrupt. Right has been replaced with wrong, and wrong is now the new right. Infanticide and abortion, assisted suicide, gay marriage, pornography, sexting, gender identity, euthanasia, sex slavery, date rape, road rage, obscenity, obsession with self, greed, cruelty, the glorification of violence through video games and rap music . . . the evidence is overwhelming that there seems to be no regard for holiness or purity.

The distressing thing I've observed is that there seems to be less and less regard for purity within the church! The church, generally speaking, seems to be absorbing the world around us instead of separating from it. The result is that the holiness of God is not always reflected in the way Christians think, live, speak, and act. Yet we are clearly commanded to "be holy as He is holy" (1 Peter 1:15). And we are warned that without holiness, no one will see the Lord. (Hebrews 12:14)

God takes sin seriously. It's time we did too. This week we will focus on the characteristic that is so much a part of the Spirit of God it's reflected in His name . . . the *Holy* Spirit.

STEP 1
Read God's Word
(Look at the Passage.)

STEP 2
What Does God's Word Say?
(List the Facts.)

Acts 5:1–6

1 Now a man named Ananias, together with his wife Sapphira, also sold a piece of property.

2 With his wife's full knowledge he kept back part of the money for himself, but brought the rest and put it at the apostles' feet.

3 Then Peter said, "Ananias, how is it that Satan has so filled your heart that you have lied to the Holy Spirit and have kept for yourself some of the money you received for the land?

4 Didn't it belong to you before it was sold? And after it was sold, wasn't the money at your disposal? What made you think of doing such a thing? You have not lied just to human beings but to God."

5 When Ananias heard this, he fell down and died. And great fear seized all who heard what had happened.

6 Then some young men came forward, wrapped up his body, and carried him out and buried him.

STEP 3
What Does God's
Word Mean?
(Learn the Lessons.)

STEP 4
What Does God's Word
Mean in My Life?
(Listen to His Voice.)

STEP 5: Live in Obedient Response to God's Word   *Date:* _____
(What will you do about what God has said?)

STEP 1	**STEP 2**
Read God's Word	What Does God's Word Say?
(Look at the Passage.)	*(List the Facts.)*

Acts 5:7–11

7 About three hours later his wife came in,
   not knowing what had happened.

8 Peter asked her, "Tell me, is this the price you
   and Ananias got for the land?" "Yes" she said,
   "that is the price."

9 Peter said to her, "How could you conspire to
   test the Spirit of the Lord? Listen! The feet of
   the men who buried your husband are at the
   door, and they will carry you out also."

10 At that moment she fell down at his feet and
   died. Then the young men came in and, finding
   her dead, carried her out and buried her beside
   her husband.

11 Great fear seized the whole church and all
   who heard about these events.

STEP 3
What Does God's Word Mean?
(Learn the Lessons.)

STEP 4
What Does God's Word Mean in My Life?
(Listen to His Voice.)

SESSION 7

STEP 5: Live in Obedient Response to God's Word   *Date:* _____
(What will you do about what God has said?)

STEP 1
Read God's Word
(Look at the Passage.)

STEP 2
What Does God's Word Say?
(List the Facts.)

1 John 1:5–10

5 This is the message we have heard from him and declare to you: God is light; in him there is no darkness at all.

6 If we claim to have fellowship with him and yet walk in the darkness, we lie and do not live out the truth.

7 But if we walk in the light, as he is in the light, we have fellowship with one another, and the blood of Jesus, his Son, purifies us from all sin.

8 If we claim to be without sin, we deceive ourselves and the truth is not in us.

9 If we confess our sins, he is faithful and just and will forgive us our sins and purify us from all unrighteousness.

10 If we claim we have not sinned, we make him out to be a liar and his word is not in us.

STEP 3
What Does God's Word Mean?
(Learn the Lessons.)

STEP 4
What Does God's Word Mean in My Life?
(Listen to His Voice.)

STEP 5: Live in Obedient Response to God's Word   *Date:* _____
(What will you do about what God has said?)

STEP 1
Read God's Word
(Look at the Passage.)

Philippians 1:9–11

9 And this is my prayer: that your love may abound more and more in knowledge and depth of insight,

10 so that you may be able to discern what is best and may be pure and blameless for the day of Christ,

11 filled with the fruit of righteousness that comes through Jesus Christ—to the glory and praise of God.

STEP 2
What Does God's Word Say?
(List the Facts.)

STEP 3
What Does God's
Word Mean?
(Learn the Lessons.)

STEP 4
What Does God's Word
Mean in My Life?
(Listen to His Voice.)

STEP 5: Live in Obedient Response to God's Word   *Date:* _____
(What will you do about what God has said?)

STEP 1
Read God's Word
(Look at the Passage.)

STEP 2
What Does God's Word Say?
(List the Facts.)

1 Peter 1:13–16

13 Therefore, with minds that are alert and fully sober, set your hope on the grace to be brought to you when Jesus Christ is revealed at his coming.

14 As obedient children, do not conform to the evil desires you had when you lived in ignorance.

15 But just as he who called you is holy, so be holy in all you do;

16 for it is written: "Be holy, because I am holy."

STEP 3
What Does God's
Word Mean?
(Learn the Lessons.)

STEP 4
What Does God's Word
Mean in My Life?
(Listen to His Voice.)

STEP 5: Live in Obedient Response to God's Word   *Date:* _____
(What will you do about what God has said?)

REFLECTION

Record and journal the following from your study this week about the PURITY of the Holy Spirit.

The Scripture that stood out to you:

The lesson that stood out to you:

The one Live in Obedient Response to God's Word that you committed to this week:

What has happened to purity? Within the church? Within the lives of those who call themselves by God's name? Is the lack of purity an indication that the Holy Spirit is withdrawing Himself?

—Anne Graham Lotz, *Jesus In Me*, page 170

GROUP STUDY

Welcome to the seventh week of the *Jesus in Me* study! What a blessing to continue on this journey and to grow in faith alongside each other.

This past week may have been a bit of a challenge for some of us. Often when we consider the difference between the holiness of God and our human, sinful state we are met with some uncomfortable and troubling truths. It takes courage to see ourselves, not as we think we are or as others say we are, but as God sees us.

The purity of the Holy Spirit is our plumb line. God measures us by the holiness of His Spirit, not in comparison with others. And He commands us to be holy as He is holy. The encouraging truth is that the Holy Spirit within us takes on the responsibility of purifying our lives.

Purification is a process, so be patient with one another and in love, encourage, listen, discuss, and share for the benefit of those in your group.

WATCH VIDEO SESSION 7 (21 MINUTES)

SCRIPTURE IN THIS SESSION:
John 14:26, 1 Peter 1:16, Leviticus 11:44–45; 19:2,
John 16:8, 1 John 1:8–9

SESSION 7

Use this space to take notes if you like:

GROUP DISCUSSION QUESTIONS

1. Open your group discussion by sharing something in the video teaching that was either striking or was new to you.

2. Refer to your personal Bible studies this past week. What was one of the most significant lessons you recorded on the purity of the Holy Spirit, and why was it significant? To which verse did it relate?

3. From the list of sins, did you spot a "no-see-um" that you would be willing to share? What do you need to put in or put out of your life?

4. Have your beliefs or your understanding of what it is to be holy changed in this session? In what ways? What has most impacted your understanding of holiness?

WRAP UP

CLOSING PRAYER: Facilitator, pray over your group.

MOVING FORWARD: Review the next week's schedule on page 132.

BLESSING & ENCOURAGEMENT: Finally, close your group meeting by reading the following blessing and encouragement over them before dismissing.

May you be blessed by the care and love
of the Holy Spirit whose heart is to
transform you more into His likeness
and share his purity and holiness to the glory of God.

GOING DEEPER

To continue your study of THE PURITY OF THE HOLY SPIRIT, read *Jesus in Me: Experiencing the Holy Spirit as a Constant Companion*, Part 6 (pages 167–194).

SESSION 7

TRUSTING IN THE *Priority* OF THE HOLY SPIRIT

. . . remember that the Holy Spirit is praying for you. Specifically. Personally. With full understanding and a heart of love.

Anne Graham Lotz, *Jesus in Me*, page 223

WEEKLY SCHEDULE

DAY 1   3-Question Study—John 4:7–10

DAY 2   3-Question Study—John 4:28–30, 39, 42

DAY 3   3-Question Study—Romans 8:22–28

DAY 4   3-Question Study—1 Corinthians 2:11–16

DAY 5   3-Question Study—2 Corinthians 3:15–18

DAY 6   Reflection, Video Teaching, Group Discussion

Trusting in the *Priority* of the Holy Spirit

"I have much more to say to you, more than you can now bear. But when he, the Spirit of truth, comes, he will guide you into all the truth. He will not speak on his own; he will speak only what he hears, and he will tell you what is yet to come."

—John 16:12–13

INDIVIDUAL STUDY INTRODUCTION

The priority of the Holy Spirit is to guide us into all truth—truth revealed in the written Word of God so that we might know the living Word of God who is Jesus . . . the truth incarnate. The purpose, the goal, and the priority of the Holy Spirit can be summed up in one word: JESUS. When we wrap our minds around the laser-like focus of the Holy Spirit, a lot of things seem to make sense, including the Bible itself. I pray that this study has not only taught you about the Holy Spirit, but opened your eyes to God's Word and your ears to His voice.

As we conclude, remember that the Holy Spirit loves you! He cares deeply about what you care about because He cares about you. It doesn't matter how small or how large your "care" is, He cares. He understands. He wants what's best for you. He desires for you to fulfill your God-given potential. He wants to ease your burden, solve your problem, comfort your broken heart, bind up your wounds, bring you through the valley of the shadow, shower you with blessing upon blessing . . . and yes, He wants to make you holy . . . because He loves you! So relax. Stop trying to impress Him. Stop working so hard to earn His love. Be open and honest and transparent. Live your life with the confidence that you are deeply, unconditionally, permanently loved by Him. You can trust Him. Just trust Him.

STEP 1
Read God's Word
(Look at the Passage.)

STEP 2
What Does God's Word Say?
(List the Facts.)

John 4:7–10

7 When a Samaritan woman came to draw water, Jesus said to her, "Will you give me a drink?"

8 (His disciples had gone into town to buy food.)

9 The Samaritan woman said to him, "You are a Jew and I am a Samaritan woman. How can you ask me for a drink?" (For Jews do not associate with Samaritans.)

10 Jesus answered her, "If you knew the gift of God and who it is that asks you for a drink, you would have asked him and he would have given you living water."

STEP 3
What Does God's
Word Mean?
(Learn the Lessons.)

STEP 4
What Does God's Word
Mean in My Life?
(Listen to His Voice.)

STEP 5: Live in Obedient Response to God's Word   *Date:* _____
(What will you do about what God has said?)

STEP 1
Read God's Word
(Look at the Passage.)

STEP 2
What Does God's Word Say?
(List the Facts.)

John 4:28–30, 39, 42

28 Then, leaving her water jar, the woman went back to the town and said to the people,

29 "Come, see a man who told me everything I ever did. Could this be the Messiah?"

30 They came out of the town and made their way toward him.

39 Many of the Samaritans from that town believed in him because of the woman's testimony, "He told me everything I ever did."

42 They said to the woman, "We no longer believe just because of what you said; now we have heard for ourselves, and we know that this man really is the Savior of the world."

STEP 3
What Does God's
Word Mean?
(Learn the Lessons.)

STEP 4
What Does God's Word
Mean in My Life?
(Listen to His Voice.)

STEP 5: Live in Obedient Response to God's Word   *Date:* _____
(What will you do about what God has said?)

STEP 1
Read God's Word
(Look at the Passage.)

STEP 2
What Does God's Word Say?
(List the Facts.)

Romans 8:22–28

22 We know that the whole creation has been groaning as in the pains of childbirth right up to the present time.

23 Not only so, but we ourselves, who have the firstfruits of the Spirit, groan inwardly as we wait eagerly for our adoption to sonship, the redemption of our bodies.

24 For in this hope we were saved. But hope that is seen is no hope at all. Who hopes for what they already have?

25 But if we hope for what we do not yet have, we wait for it patiently.

26 In the same way, the Spirit helps us in our weakness. We do not know what we ought to pray for, but the Spirit himself intercedes for us through wordless groans.

27 And he who searches our hearts knows the mind of the Spirit, because the Spirit intercedes for God's people in accordance with the will of God.

28 And we know that in all things God works for the good of those who love him, who have been called according to his purpose.

STEP 3
What Does God's
Word Mean?
(Learn the Lessons.)

STEP 4
What Does God's Word
Mean in My Life?
(Listen to His Voice.)

STEP 5: Live in Obedient Response to God's Word   *Date:* _____
(What will you do about what God has said?)

STEP 1
Read God's Word
(Look at the Passage.)

STEP 2
What Does God's Word Say?
(List the Facts.)

1 Corinthians 2:11–16

11 For who knows a person's thoughts except
their own spirit within them? In the same way
no one knows the thoughts of God except
the Spirit of God.

12 What we have received is not the spirit of the
world, but the Spirit who is from God, so that
we may understand what God has freely given us.

13 This is what we speak, not in words taught us by
human wisdom but in words taught by the Spirit,
explaining spiritual realities with Spirit-taught words.

14 The person without the Spirit does not accept the
things that come from the Spirit of God but
considers them foolishness, and cannot understand
them because they are discerned only through the Spirit.

15 The person with the Spirit makes judgments
about all things, but such a person is not subject
to merely human judgments,

16 for, "Who has known the mind of the Lord so as
to instruct him?" But we have the mind of Christ.

STEP 3
What Does God's
Word Mean?
(Learn the Lessons.)

STEP 4
What Does God's Word
Mean in My Life?
(Listen to His Voice.)

STEP 5: Live in Obedient Response to God's Word   *Date:* _____
(What will you do about what God has said?)

STEP 1
Read God's Word
(Look at the Passage.)

STEP 2
What Does God's Word Say?
(List the Facts.)

2 Corinthians 3:15–18

15 Even to this day when Moses is read,
a veil covers their hearts.

16 But whenever anyone turns to the
Lord, the veil is taken away.

17 Now the Lord is the Spirit, and where
the Spirit of the Lord is, there is freedom.

18 And we all, who with unveiled faces
contemplate the Lord's glory, are being
transformed into his image, with
ever-increasing glory, which comes
from the Lord, who is the Spirit.

STEP 3
What Does God's
Word Mean?
(Learn the Lessons.)

STEP 4
What Does God's Word
Mean in My Life?
(Listen to His Voice.)

STEP 5: Live in Obedient Response to God's Word   *Date:* _____
(What will you do about what God has said?)

REFLECTION

Record and journal the following from your study this week about the PRIORITY of the Holy Spirit.

The Scripture that stood out to you:

The lesson that stood out to you:

The one Live in Obedient Response to God's Word that you committed to this week:

Jesus is the reason for everything that exists,

including you and me. He is our ultimate purpose,

our ultimate goal, and our ultimate priority.

If your life's purpose, goal, and priorities

are about anything less than Jesus only,

anything other than Jesus only,

anything more than Jesus only,

then there is a disconnect between you

and the Holy Spirit. Because, remember,

the Holy Spirit's ultimate purpose is to glorify Jesus,

His ultimate goal is to make Jesus known to you

and to me, and His priority is to

guide us into all truth as

He transforms us into the image of Jesus.

—Anne Graham Lotz, *Jesus in Me*, page 238

GROUP STUDY

W ELCOME TO THE FINAL WEEK of our Jesus in Me Bible study!

What difference has this study made in your habits? Your daily or weekly schedule? Your thinking? What has made it worth your time and effort?

Share with your group what you have enjoyed most about this group study. As you gather this week, take time to express your gratitude for all the Holy Spirit has taught you, shown you, and revealed to you. Take a moment to reflect on the fact that the Holy Spirit is Jesus. In you! He will be your constant companion as you leave this study, and one day will present you faultless before the Father. To the praise of His glory!

WATCH VIDEO SESSION 8 (21:30 MINUTES)

SCRIPTURE IN THIS SESSION
Romans 8:26, Ephesians 4:30, John 16:13–14,
Genesis 1:2–3, John 1:14, Colossians 1:16, Genesis 2–5, 18, 32,
Joshua 5–6, Daniel 3, Isaiah 43:2, Psalm 23:4,
Isaiah 6, Ezekiel, Luke 2, 24, Revelation 19

Use this space to take notes if you like:

GROUP DISCUSSION QUESTIONS

1. Open your group discussion by sharing something in the video that was either striking or was new to you.

2. Refer to your personal Bible studies this past week. What was one of the most significant lessons you recorded on the priority of the Holy Spirit, and why was it significant? To which verse did it relate? Without the Spirit's clarity, how does the world view Jesus?

3. Turn to John 16:13 in your Bibles. Discuss practical ways we can apply John 16:13 to a person's struggle to understand God's Word.

4. Who is the subject of the Bible according to Luke 24:27? Why is this so relevant to our understanding of the Bible? What are we missing if we overlook this one key fact?

WRAP UP

CLOSING PRAYER: Facilitator, pray over your group.

BLESSING & ENCOURAGEMENT: Then, close your group meeting by reading the following blessing and encouragement over them before dismissing.

May the Holy Spirit guide you into all truth,
keep you from distraction, doubt, discouragement,
and disobedience. May you continue to know Jesus,
love Jesus, and trust Jesus so that you
can bring glory to Him.

What are some ways you can tell others who the Holy Spirit is? Consider hosting a Bible study group yourself using this curriculum. Who can you invite? Who do you know that would benefit from this study?

GOING DEEPER

To continue your study of THE PRIORITY OF THE HOLY SPIRIT, read *Jesus in Me: Experiencing the Holy Spirit as a Constant Companion*, Part 7 and Conclusion (pages 195–239).

SESSION 8

CLOSING PRAYER

My prayer for you as you conclude your study of Jesus in Me is taken from
Colossians 1:9–10:

> *For this reason,*
>
> *since the day we heard about you,*
>
> *we have not stopped praying for you.*
>
> *We continually ask God to fill you with the knowledge of his will*
>
> *through all the wisdom and understanding that the Spirit gives,*
>
> *so that you may live a life worthy of the Lord and please him in every way:*
>
> *bearing fruit in every good work,*
>
> *growing in the knowledge of God . . .*

May God richly bless you as you continue to read your Bible, listening for His
voice.

Sincerely,

Anne

Write your own prayer of commitment here.

CONTENTS

THANK YOU

THANK YOU FOR SERVING AS THE FACILITATOR for the participants who will join you in this study. While I will have the privilege of speaking to them through the video series, your leadership is essential. Your thoughtful and loving guidance will encourage them to consistently do their Bible study during the week and feel comfortable sharing their discoveries in your group. Please be assured that I, and others on this curriculum development team, have been praying for you.

I thank my God every time I remember you. In all my prayers for all of you,
I always pray with joy because of your partnership in the gospel from the first day until now, being
confident of this, that he who began a good work in you will carry it on to completion until the day of
Christ Jesus (Philippians 1:3–6).

As you lead others to discover the Holy Spirit as their constant companion, I pray that you will encourage each other to effectively share who the Holy Spirit is: Jesus in me. And in you.

For His Glory,

FOR STARTERS

Please take a few minutes to read this helpful information before you begin the *Jesus in Me* study. It should answer most of the questions you may have.

WHAT'S ON THE VIDEOS?

The accompanying videos feature the following components:

- An interactive workshop in session 1 led by Anne Graham Lotz that describes the Bible study method participants will be using.
- Seven additional video sessions with Anne that focus on learning about the Holy Spirit.

WHAT OTHER MATERIALS ARE NEEDED?

The following materials will be needed for a successful small group time:

- A computer with monitor or a television with a DVD player
- A watch, clock, or cellphone with alarm (to monitor the time)
- *Jesus in Me* Study Guide (one per group member)
- *Jesus in Me* Video Study
- A Bible (one per group member)
- Pens or pencils (enough for everyone)
- Optional: *Jesus in Me* book by Anne Graham Lotz (recommended for leaders, but optional for participants)

GOOD TO KNOW

Here are a few additional items to keep in mind as you lead your group:

- **Your Role as Facilitator:** As the facilitator, your role is to take care of your guests by managing the behind-the-scenes details so that when everyone arrives, they can just enjoy their time together. Your role is not to answer all the questions or reteach the content—the video and study guide will do much of the work. You want to guide the group and make it a place where people can process, question, and reflect on the Bible readings and the teachings.

- **Setting and Time:** This study can work equally well in church or home groups. The first session is planned to be 90 minutes in length, while the subsequent sessions are approximately 60 minutes. In more formal, time-sensitive church settings, you will likely need to follow the time frames provided in the session outline more closely in order to finish all the content. In less formal home settings, you can "round off" time frames and still end up with about an hour of study material. In either case, remember these are suggested time frames and are open to adjustment as you see fit.

- **Hospitality:** Regardless of where you conduct the study, create an environment that is conducive to sharing and learning. Make sure there is enough comfortable seating for everyone and, if possible, arrange the seats in a semicircle so everyone can see the video. This will make the transition between the video and group conversation more natural. Consider offering simple refreshments to create a welcoming atmosphere, and make sure your media technology is working properly before the session begins.

WEEKLY PREPARATION

As the facilitator, there are a few things you many want to do to prepare for each meeting:

- **Read through the lesson:** This will help you to become familiar with the content and know how to structure the discussion times.
- **Decide which questions you want to discuss:** You may not be able to cover every question in the group discussion section. Select the questions ahead of time that you absolutely want the group to discuss in depth.
- **Be familiar with the questions you want to discuss:** When the group meets you will be watching the clock, so make sure you are familiar with the study questions you have selected.
- **Pray for your group:** Pray for your group members by name throughout the week and ask God to lead them as they study His Word.
- **Bring extra supplies to your meeting:** The group members should bring their own pens for writing notes, but it's a good idea to have extras available for those who forget. You may also want to bring additional paper and Bibles.

GROUP DYNAMICS

Leading a group is highly rewarding, but that doesn't mean you will not encounter any challenges along the way. Discussions can get off track. Group members may not be sensitive to the ideas of others. Some may express comments that result in disagreements. To help ease this strain on you and the group, consider the following ground rules:

- **Off topic:** When someone raises a question or comment that is off the main topic, suggest you deal with it another time, or, if you feel led to go in that direction, let the group know you will be spending some time discussing it.
- **Don't know the answer:** If someone asks a question you don't know how to

answer, admit it and move on. At your discretion, feel free to invite group members to comment on questions that call for personal experience.

- **Dominating discussion:** If you find one or two people are dominating the discussion time, direct questions to others in the group. Outside the group time, ask the more dominating members to help you draw out the quieter ones. Work to make them a part of the solution instead of the problem.

- **Disagreements:** When a disagreement occurs, encourage group members to process the matter in love. Have those on opposite sides restate what they heard the other side say about the matter, and then invite each side to evaluate if that perception is accurate. It's most important that the answers given are based on the passages of Scripture studied.

When these situations arise, guide your group to follow the words from the Bible: "Love one another" (John 13:34), "As far as it depends on you, live at peace with everyone" (Romans 12:18), and "Be quick to listen, slow to speak and slow to become angry" (James 1:19).

BIBLE STUDY WORKSHOP

BIBLE STUDY WORKSHOP

For the best experience in facilitating this study, it's important to preview the video for session 1 and complete all the written exercises in this study guide prior to leading your group. Familiarize yourself with the session outline and gather the necessary materials. Pray for the participants by name (if known). Pray Ephesians 1:17–18 for them, that God will open their hearts to His Word and they will get to know Him better as a result of the Spirit's revelation.

SESSION OUTLINE (90 MINUTES)

I. Introduction/Opening Prayer (5 minutes)

II. Explanation of Bible Study Sessions (5 minutes)

III. Video Teaching and Group Work (70 minutes)

    A. Opening and Teaching on Steps 1–2 (13 minutes)

    B. Group Work on Steps 1–2 (5 minutes)

    C. Review of Steps 1–2 and Teaching on Step 3 (2 minutes)

    D. Group Work on Step 3 (15 minutes)

    E. Review of Step 3 and Teaching on Step 4 (13 minutes)

    F. Group Work on Step 4 (5 minutes)

  G. Review of Step 4 and Teaching on Step 5 (12 minutes)

  H. Group Work on Step 5 (5 minutes)

 IV. Wrapping Up and Next Steps (10 minutes)

INTRODUCTION/OPENING PRAYER (5 MINUTES)

Take a few moments as this opening session begins to introduce yourself to anyone in the group you do not know and give your contact information. If it can be done quickly, ask the participants to introduce themselves. It may be helpful in a larger group to provide nametags. To save time, you can have the nametags pre-printed with their names on one side, and your name and contact information on the other side. Ensure the participants have a copy of the study guide. Pray that God would use the coming hour to help everyone present to become more effective students and doers of His Word.

EXPLANATION OF BIBLE STUDY SESSIONS (5 MINUTES)

Explain that this first session in *Jesus in Me* is unique, as Anne will describe a method for studying the Bible that they will use during their personal quiet time throughout the study. During this opening session, which will be approximately 90 minutes in length, the group members will watch the video and complete the work found on pages 6–9.

VIDEO TEACHING AND GROUP WORK (70 MINUTES)

Show the video, following the instructions given by Anne during the session. Note that you will be stopping the video periodically for the participants to complete each of the steps.

WRAPPING UP AND NEXT STEPS (10 MINUTES)

Tell the group members that they will begin to explore the Holy Spirit in sessions 2–8. Refer group members to the Individual Bible Study found on page 11, and ask them to complete the studies before the next session. Close your time in prayer.

LOVING THE *Person*
OF THE HOLY SPIRIT

P REVIEW THE VIDEO BEFORE YOUR MEETING and complete all the written exercises in this guide. Familiarize yourself with the session outline and gather the necessary materials. Remember also to pray for the participants who will be attending.

SESSION OUTLINE (60 MINUTES)

REVIEW OF PRE-SESSION BIBLE STUDY (15 MINUTES)

Welcome any new participants, and then refer the group to their notes on pages 14–24. As time allows, have one member share the facts he or she drew from each verse (Step 2). Then have several different members share the following:

- The lessons they learned from each verse (Step 3).
- The most meaningful question they wrote out in response to Step 4, citing the verse on which the question was based.
- Their outstanding takeaway in Step 5.

VIDEO TEACHING (18 MINUTES)

Watch the teaching video for session 2. Refer the group members to page 27 and remind them there is space to take notes.

GROUP DISCUSSION (17 MINUTES)

Refer to the Group Discussion questions on page 28 to stimulate discussion on the topics presented during the video teaching. Ask the group members to share any personal encouragement, challenge, or inspiration they received as they watched.

WRAP UP AND GO DEEPER (10 MINUTES)

Conclude by praying over your group. Review the next week's schedule on page 32 and finally close your group meeting by reading the blessing and encouragement on page 29. Remind them to read the passage and complete the studies before the next session. Close in prayer.

ENJOYING THE *Presence* OF THE HOLY SPIRIT

PREVIEW THE VIDEO BEFORE YOUR MEETING and complete all the written exercises in this guide. Familiarize yourself with the session outline and gather the necessary materials. Remember also to pray for the participants who will be attending.

SESSION OUTLINE (60 MINUTES)

REVIEW OF PRE-SESSION BIBLE STUDY (15 MINUTES)

Welcome any new participants, and then refer the group to their notes on pages 34–44. As time allows, have one member share the facts he or she drew from each verse (Step 2). Then have several different members share the following:

- The lessons they learned from each verse (Step 3).
- The most meaningful question they wrote out in response to Step 4, citing the verse on which the question was based.
- Their outstanding takeaway in Step 5.

VIDEO TEACHING (17:30 MINUTES)

Watch the teaching video for session 3. Refer the group members to the outline on page 47 and remind them there is space to take notes.

GROUP DISCUSSION (17 MINUTES)

Refer to the Group Discussion questions on page 48 to stimulate discussion on the topics presented during the video teaching. Ask the group members to share any personal encouragement, challenge, or inspiration they received as they watched.

WRAP UP AND GO DEEPER (10 MINUTES)

Conclude by praying over your group. Review the next week's schedule on page 52 and finally close your group meeting by reading the blessing and encouragement on page 49. Remind them to read the passage and complete the studies before the next session. Close in prayer.

RELYING ON THE
Power OF THE HOLY SPIRIT

P REVIEW THE VIDEO BEFORE YOUR MEETING and complete all the written exercises in this guide. Familiarize yourself with the session outline and gather the necessary materials. Remember also to pray for the participants who will be attending.

SESSION OUTLINE (60 MINUTES)

REVIEW OF PRE-SESSION BIBLE STUDY (15 MINUTES)

Welcome any new participants, and then refer the group to their notes on pages 54–64. As time allows, have one member share the facts he or she drew from each verse (Step 2). Then have several different members share the following:

- The lessons they learned from each verse (Step 3).
- The most meaningful question they wrote out in response to Step 4, citing the verse on which the question was based.
- Their outstanding takeaway in Step 5.

VIDEO TEACHING (17 MINUTES)

Watch the teaching video for session 4. Refer the group members to page 67 and remind them there is space to take notes.

GROUP DISCUSSION (17 MINUTES)

Refer to the Group Discussion questions on page 68 to stimulate discussion on the topics presented during the video teaching. Ask the group members to share any personal encouragement, challenge, or inspiration they received as they watched.

WRAP UP AND GO DEEPER (10 MINUTES)

Conclude by praying over your group. Review the next week's schedule on page 72 and finally close your group meeting by reading the blessing and encouragement on page 69. Remind them to read the passage and complete the studies before the next session. Close in prayer.

EMBRACING THE
Purpose OF THE HOLY SPIRIT

P REVIEW THE VIDEO BEFORE YOUR MEETING and complete all the written exercises in this guide. Familiarize yourself with the session outline and gather the necessary materials. Remember also to pray for the participants who will be attending.

SESSION OUTLINE (60 MINUTES)

REVIEW OF PRE-SESSION BIBLE STUDY (15 MINUTES)

Welcome any new participants, and then refer the group to their notes on pages 74–84. As time allows, have one member share the facts he or she drew from each verse (Step 2). Then have several different members share the following:

- The lessons they learned from each verse (Step 3).
- The most meaningful question they wrote out in response to Step 4, citing the verse on which the question was based.
- Their outstanding takeaway in Step 5.

VIDEO TEACHING (15 MINUTES)

Watch the teaching video for session 5. Refer the group members to page 87 and remind them there is space to take notes.

GROUP DISCUSSION (17 MINUTES)

Refer to the Group Discussion questions on page 88 to stimulate discussion on the topics presented during the video teaching. Ask the group members to share any personal encouragement, challenge, or inspiration they received as they watched.

WRAP UP AND GO DEEPER (10 MINUTES)

Conclude by praying over your group. Review the next week's schedule on page 92 and finally close your group meeting by reading the blessing and encouragement on page 89. Remind them to read the passage and complete the studies before the next session. Close in prayer.

LIVING BY THE
Precepts OF THE HOLY SPIRIT

P REVIEW THE VIDEO BEFORE YOUR MEETING and complete all the written exercises in this guide. Familiarize yourself with the session outline and gather the necessary materials. Remember also to pray for the participants who will be attending.

SESSION OUTLINE (60 MINUTES)

REVIEW OF PRE-SESSION BIBLE STUDY (15 MINUTES)

Welcome any new participants, and then refer the group to their notes on pages 94–104. As time allows, have one member share the facts he or she drew from each verse (Step 2). Then have several different members share the following:

- The lessons they learned from each verse (Step 3).
- The most meaningful question they wrote out in response to Step 4, citing the verse on which the question was based.
- Their outstanding takeaway in Step 5.

VIDEO TEACHING (16:30 MINUTES)

Watch the teaching video for session 6. Refer the group members to the outline on page 107 and remind them there is space to take notes.

GROUP DISCUSSION (17 MINUTES)

Refer to the Group Discussion questions on page 108 to stimulate discussion on the topics presented during the video teaching. Ask the group members to share any personal encouragement, challenge, or inspiration they received as they watched.

WRAP UP AND GO DEEPER (10 MINUTES)

Conclude by praying over your group. Review the next week's schedule on page 112 and finally close your group meeting by reading the blessing and encouragement on page 109. Remind them to read the passage and complete the studies before the next session. Close in prayer.

REFLECTING THE
Purity OF THE HOLY SPIRIT

P REVIEW THE VIDEO BEFORE YOUR MEETING and complete all the written exercises in this guide. Familiarize yourself with the session outline and gather the necessary materials. Remember also to pray for the participants who will be attending.

SESSION OUTLINE (60 MINUTES)

REVIEW OF PRE-SESSION BIBLE STUDY (15 MINUTES)

Welcome any new participants, and then refer the group to their notes on pages 114–124. As time allows, have one member share the facts he or she drew from each verse (Step 2). Then have several different members share the following:

- The lessons they learned from each verse (Step 3).
- The most meaningful question they wrote out in response to Step 4, citing the verse on which the question was based.
- Their outstanding takeaway in Step 5.

VIDEO TEACHING (16:30 MINUTES)

Watch the teaching video for session 7. Refer the group members to page 127 and remind them there is space to take notes.

GROUP DISCUSSION (17 MINUTES)

Refer to the Group Discussion questions on page 128 to stimulate discussion on the topics presented during the video teaching. Ask the group members to share any personal encouragement, challenge, or inspiration they received as they watched.

WRAP UP AND GO DEEPER (10 MINUTES)

Conclude by praying over your group. Review the next week's schedule on page 132 and finally close your group meeting by reading the blessing and encouragement on page 129. Remind them to read the passage and complete the studies before the next session. Close in prayer.

TRUSTING IN THE
Priority OF THE HOLY SPIRIT

Preview the video before your meeting and complete all the written exercises in this guide. Familiarize yourself with the session outline and gather the necessary materials. Remember also to pray for the participants who will be attending.

SESSION OUTLINE (60 MINUTES)

REVIEW OF PRE-SESSION BIBLE STUDY (15 MINUTES)

Welcome any new participants, and then refer the group to their notes on pages 134–144. As time allows, have one member share the facts he or she drew from each verse (Step 2). Then have several different members share the following:

- The lessons they learned from each verse (Step 3).
- The most meaningful question they wrote out in response to Step 4, citing the verse on which the question was based.
- Their outstanding takeaway in Step 5.

VIDEO TEACHING (21:30 MINUTES)

Watch the teaching video for session 8. Refer the group members to page 132 and remind them there is space to take notes.

GROUP DISCUSSION (17 MINUTES)

Refer to the Group Discussion questions on page 148 to stimulate discussion on the topics presented during the video teaching. Ask the group members to share any personal encouragement, challenge, or inspiration they received as they watched.

WRAP UP AND GO DEEPER (10 MINUTES)

Conclude by praying over your group. Take the opportunity to meet again soon to discuss some of the new things the Holy Spirit is teaching you.

Pray too for each other to effectively share with people outside the group about who the Holy Spirit is: Jesus in me. And in you.

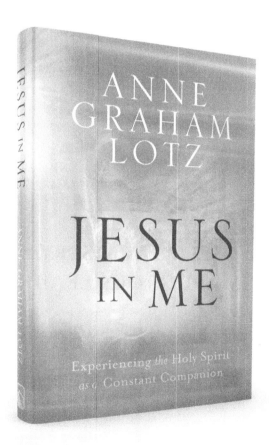

BIBLE STUDY SOURCE
for women

powered by ChurchSource

Connecting you with the best in

BIBLE STUDY RESOURCES

from many of the world's

MOST TRUSTED BIBLE TEACHERS

JENNIE
ALLEN

JADA
EDWARDS

ANNE
GRAHAM LOTZ

CHRYSTAL
EVANS HURST

Providing

WOMEN'S MINISTRY AND
SMALL GROUP LEADERS

with the INSPIRATION, ENCOURAGEMENT,
AND RESOURCES to grow your ministry

powered by ChurchSource

join our
COMMUNITY

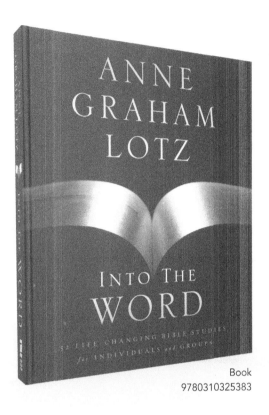